3 Day Guide to Provence

A 72-hour definitive guide on what to see, eat and enjoy in Provence, France

3 DAY GUIDES

Copyright © 2015 BeautyBodyStyle, LLC

All rights reserved. No part of this book may be reproduced in any form or by any electronic or mechanical means including information storage and retrieval systems – except in the case of brief quotations in articles or reviews – without the permission in writing from its publisher.

Although the author and publisher have made every effort to ensure that the information in this book was correct at press time, the author and publisher do not assume and hereby disclaim any liability to any party for any loss, damage, or disruption caused by errors or omissions, whether such errors or omissions result from negligence, accident, or any other cause.

Image use under CC-BY License via Flickr

Photo Credits:

Provence Landscape. Photo credit: François Philipp

Provence Side Street, Bread & Wine. Photo credit: Christopher Michel

ISBN: 1507506082
ISBN-13: 978-1507506080

"Our happiest moments as tourists always seem to come when we stumble upon one thing while in pursuit of something else." — Lawrence Block.

CONTENTS

1	Introduction to Provence	1
2	Avignon	13
3	Arles	23
4	Aix-en-Provence	34
5	Best Places (Eat, Wine & Dine)	39
6	Best Places to Stay	46
7	Recommended Places to Visit	50
	Conclusion	52
	More from This Author	54

1 INTRODUCTION TO PROVENCE

Provence Region. Photo credit: <u>Christopher Michel</u>

Lost for words... this is the exact description that befits a region like Provence. It is so unique, whipping up phrases with the right adjectives will always fall short for what is "real". The string of colors, whether bursting or subdued, will captivate, move and touch your core. It offers a kaleidoscope of discoveries. No wonder great artists like Renoir, Cezanne, Van Gogh, Picasso and many others found their inspirations here... where time is of no essence, you won't even notice it passing by.

The charm of this region is so admirable. It is so unique you can feel it piercing your very soul. It is very transparent and is clearly mirrored on every street, in every nook and cranny. It is etched on every place that you will see and visit. You will feel it on every person that you will encounter and meet. You will quickly discover that France is an intriguing country with an amazing past.

Let your thoughts sway away with the beauty of Provence. Fill your imagination with the richness of its history. Wander away in a place of meandering beauty of scenic landscapes and colorful flower fields. Be out with olive trees, lavender, and vineyards.

This is the place for the beauty and bees, the flowers and the trees. Where clear light shines and pours through meadows, reflecting different hues that will play with your imagination. When darkness descends, it becomes all the more exciting as the whole scenario unfolds for the perfect location where you can drink and dine under the stars.

The romance of Provence is quintessential, it is poetic, with a classic twist.

This will be a trip that will take you to a wonderful world of discoveries. You will be en route to a journey of a glorious era when remarkable civilizations existed, traces of which still stands proudly on this province. Travel down the path to a thousand or more years before us.

Have you imagined being in a place where colors playfully intermingle with nature? A place full of art and inspirations? A world of charm and romance? This…. is Provence.

History

Located in the Southeastern part of France, this region is bordered by the Rhone River on the west, Italy on the east and by the Mediterranean Sea on the South. It was the earliest inhabited place in Europe dating back to Paleolithic age. Early settlers were farmers and warriors. Traces of the early civilizations can still be found in many parts of Provence

Due to its geographical location, part of the region's history shows it was the first Roman declared province beyond the Alps in the early 13th century and called this region Provincia Romana. They were under the rule of the Counts of Provence until 1481 when it became a province of the Kings of France and has been a part of France for more than 500 years now.

Ligures and Celts

The region was also inhabited by Ligures between the 10th and 4th century BC. This group was of uncertain origins but may have been the descendants of Neolithic people. They were more into hunting and war, invading Italy in the 4th century. Traces of these inhabitants, like their primitive stone shelters called "Bories" and rock carvings can still be found all over the region.

Celtics came into Provence between the 8th and 5th centuries BC. These tribes had remarkable weapons made of iron. Both Celts and Ligurians shared the territory of Provence, each tribe settled in the Alpine Valley and along the river. They built hilltop forts and settlements.

Greeks

7th century is the time when Greeks came into the coast of Provence. They came from the island of Rhodes. The first permanent Greek settlement was Massalia, now known as Marseille. The most famous citizen of Massalia was Phyteas, the great mathematician, astronomer and navigator.

Romans

2nd century saw the arrival of the Romans in the region to help them out against the Ligures. In 125 BC, they established permanent settlements in Provence and in 122 BC, they've built a new town, Aquae Sextiae, now known as Aix-en-Provence. The Pax Romana in Provence lasted until the middle of the 3rd century. Germanic tribes invaded the province in the later centuries and at the end of the 5th century, Roman power in Provence ended. With the waning of the Roman Empire, Germanic tribes entered Provence. They ruled the region until the 9th century when Provence was ruled by three different dynasties of Counts, the Catalan rulers of Barcelona, the German rulers of the Holy Romas Empire and the Angevin Kings of France.

Papal seat officially transferred to Avignon in 1309

and was transferred back to Rome in 1423. Palais de Papes became the official papal residence and is considered to be the largest gothic palace in Europe.

The Black Plague of 1348-1350 was one of the most terrible times not just in Provence but in all of Europe. It killed thousands of people in the region.

The French Revolution

Provence also played an important part in the French Revolution. It produced some of the prominent figures who played important roles in this historic period. "Le Marseillaise", the most memorable song sung on the streets of Paris, the most popular song of the Revolution, originally came from Provence. It is now the National Anthem of France.

The French Revolution was a bloody and violent uprising in Provence as it was in the other parts of France. This has been one of the most tragic events in their history. Their burning sense of nationalism left a mark in their history. In 1795, calm and peace was eventually restored as Napoleon rose to power.

Today, Provence of the 20th century is marked with economic development and population growth while never ceasing to preserve and maintain their natural landscape and culture.

Climate

Provence has a subtropical climate. It is oftentimes described as a typical "Mediterranean" weather –

with summers that are sunny, hot and dry. Winters are mild with very little snow and abundant sunshine. Most rainy winters are cold but don't have freezing temperatures.

The complexity of its seasons may seem to be a bit odd but it has something to do with its geographical location. It is lying directly below the Alps, along the Mediterranean and on the Rhone Valley.

This is a favored climate where the weather fronts coming from the north are hindered by the mountains. The climate on the coastal strip is particularly mild and this region has the mildest winters of any place in France.

Provence has the driest region also in the entire country. The dryness of the climate is due to the effect of the "Mistral" wind. These are cold, dry winds blown down from the Rhone Valley and often reaches over a hundred kilometers per hour. These winds are brought about when two weather systems are pushed south (high pressure over Western Europe and depression over Central Europe) as they reach the Western edge of the Alps, surging down the Rhone Valley towards Provence. They generally bring clear skies, but not warm temperatures.

A strong winter Mistral can send temperatures plunging down to sub-zero or just above zero, without the snow. Generally, Provence is an ideal tourist destination any time of the year depending on the type of vacation that one would prefer. All-year round, Provence offers a lot of activities that you can enjoy.

Seasons

Winter – December to February

Most museums and natural sites or Provence are open all-year round. This is also a perfect time to enjoy the place sans the heavy crowds. Climate is very mild and is a great time for a trip to Provence. Popular attractions such as theatres, museums, palaces and others are open with fewer crowds (no need to stand in line!). This is also the best time to avail the winter sales where you can get the best deals.

Spring – March to May

Spring as in many other places spells "renewed" exuberance after the dreary winter months. It is the perfect season to enjoy trees starting to bloom and flowers slowly showing up their buds.

The prices are still moderate, as the colors change with the few rays of sunshine slipping' through.

Summer – June to August

The warm weather of summer is perfect for any fun-filled activity in Provence. The beaches are of course, the prime destination. You just need to bear in mind that since this is the peak season for tourists, some places may be jam-packed with visitors. The months of June and July are where you can bask on the beauty of nature at its best in Provence highlighted of course by the famous

Lavender fields where the flowers are in full bloom.

Fall – September to November

These are the months when the green leaves turn into amber and orange. Weather is still hot but mild. September and October are the perfect season when there are a few tourists but most establishments offers lower prices.

The days are sunny and breezy and the temperature is warm but not too hot.

Best Time to Visit

It will be hard to determine the exact season which will be best for a trip to Provence. It may actually depend on whether you would like to spend an idyllic, quiet vacation all on your own – best months to go will be on the spring months of March to May, winter months of December to January or be there during Autumn. But if you would opt to experience the peak of the season with all the hustle and bustle of the crowd, summer months will surely beckon you.

Language

Provencal is the language spoken in Provence. It is a dialect of the Occitan language. Occitan is referred to as the Romance language and is spoken in Southern France, Italy's Occitan Valleys, Monaco and Spain's Val d'Aran. These regions are known collectively as the Occitania. Today, Provencal is known as the dialect spoken in Provence. In the beginning of the 20th century, this dialect was generally replaced with French. Today, Provencal is still being taught in schools and universities in the region but is spoken by just a minority of people, mostly the elders.

Getting In

Marseille-Provence

One of the two major airports in Provence, it is located 25km northeast of Marseille. It has regular flights to major destinations in Europe, including a number in the UK and Ireland. There are frequent flights to 20 French airports and 2-3 flights daily between Marseille and most European cities. It also serves as a hub for flights to and from North Africa, with regular flights to Algeria, Morocco and Tunisia.

Nice- Cote d'Azur

This is the second largest airport in Provence. Located 6km west of Nice, this is France's second-largest airport. It has regular flights to major international and French destinations, including many in UK and Ireland. There are daily flights between Nice and most European cities.

There are also several other airports in Provence which include Nimes-Garons, which is 15km south of Nimes which has daily flights to London plus flights to other destinations in Europe and the Toulon-Hyeres, a small airport 25km east of Tulon which has flights to nine European cities depending on the season. There are daily flights to Paris year-round and seasonal flights to the UK.

Getting Around

Southern France has one the best transportation systems in Europe particularly their bus and railway systems. There are several ways to explore Provence. Whatever option you may choose to take, you are guaranteed to have the best Provence experience as you take the tour around the region.

By car:

One of the best ways to tour the region is by car. It will give you the freedom of time and the luxury of stopping over on side spots. Road trips to countryside and the villages will be a breeze but parking may sometimes pose some challenges. This is particularly true in Arles as there are only a few spaces to be found in the area. Most towns only have parking areas out of the center, so hiring a vehicle may not excuse you from steep pathways and stairs.

By bike:

One unique way of exploring the countryside will be on two-wheels. You just need to consider first the weather. Some places have occasional slopes and small hills, mostly back roads and a few light-traffic highways with flat roads. Plan a bike-friendly journey on Véloroutes (www.af3v.org) or join a cycling tour if you're feeling sociable.

By bus:

Eurolines (08 92 89 90 91; www.eurolines.com) is an association of companies forming Europe's largest international bus network. It links Provençal cities such as Nice, Marseille and Avignon with points all over western and central Europe, Scandinavia and Morocco. Most buses operate daily in summer and several times a week in winter; advance ticket purchases are necessary. Eurolines' website lists representatives in Europe. The Eurolines Pass (15-/30-day high-season pass €340/410, under 26 €260/310, cheaper mid-Sep-Jun) allows unlimited travel to 45 cities across Europe.

Linebùs (Avignon 04 90 86 88 67; Nîmes 04 66 29 50 62; Barcelona 932 65 07 00, www.linebus.com, in Spanish) links Avignon (6½ hours, €45 one-way) and Nîmes (6¼ hours, €41 one-way) with Barcelona and other cities in Spain. Children aged four to 12 receive a 50% discount.

By train:

French transport policy favors its state-owned rail system: inter-regional bus services are an alien concept. When travelling to Provence from other regions of France, it's easiest to take the train.

Thomas Cook's European Rail Timetable, updated monthly, and has a complete listing of train schedules. It's available from Thomas Cook offices worldwide and online (www.thomascookpublishing.com) for around UK£14. Another helpful resource is the info-packed website The Man in Seat 61 (www.seat61.com), which lists train timetables and travel tips for France and beyond.

You may also refer to:
http://www.beyond.fr/travel/railtravel.html

2 AVIGNON

Avignon - Place du Palais - Papal Palace. Photo credit: Elliott Brown

A 3-day trip to explore Provence can readily begin in Avignon.

Avignon is city of a rich historical past, surrounded by Medieval Walls. A number of historical palaces, museums and other structures can be found here. Avignon was home to the pope for more than 100 years in the 14th century. Today, Avignon is considered to be one of the most beautiful cities in France as it was able to retain its old world charm in mixture of a youthful city flourishing within its walls. Backstreets are still made up of cobble-stones and the pedestrian alleys are just wide enough for strolling. There's a lot of interesting attractions within this city.

You may start the day with a breakfast of warm coffee, crepe and croissant at the courtyard café inside Palais des Papes.

Papal Palace of Avignon

Known as the Great Palace of the Popes, this is a UNESCO World Heritage Site. This has been the official residence of the Pope for almost 100 years. In 1309, this has been triggered by the removal of Curia from Rome to Avignon under Pope Clement V. His successor, John XXII (Pope 1316-34) chose the palace of the Bishop of Avignon, his nephew, Arnaud de Via, as his official seat and initiated the first extensions. The palace is composed of two wings, the east and northeast wings of Palais Vieux (Old Palace) built by Benedict XII (Pope 1334-42) and the west wing of Palais Nouveau (New Palace) built by Clement VI (Pope 1342-52). Succeeding popes have made additional extensions and completions. It was also during these times that there has been a conflict and division in the Roman Catholic leadership where popes and antipopes were simultaneously elected. This conflict only ended in 1423 when the Papacy finally returned to Rome.

Today, this palace is the largest Gothic palace in Europe and it is still clearly visible on its walls, ceilings and floors. This magnificent structure has an estimated floor area of 15,000 square meters. The papal bedroom has nature-inspired motif depicted on its walls and floors. Today, you will no longer see original furnishings within this edifice but the legacy of its past is still visible through the shadows of this fortress-like structure.

Address: Palace du Palais, 84000 Avignon, France

Phone: 04 32 74 32 74

Avignon Cathedral

Known as the Cathedral of Notre-Dame des Doms, this cathedral was first built in the 12th century. Standing between Palais des Papes and Petit Palais, this structure's size humbly dwarfed between the two giant edifices. Nonetheless, this Cathedral claims its own historical importance and architectural grandeur. Not to steal the thunder from the two, it has its own distinct charm and story. In the 14th to 16th century, it was altered several times. The arch and gable on the main doorways are remains of the frescoes by Simone Martin. Baroque galleries were added in the 17th century. The gilded statue of the Virgin Mary on the tower was also added during the 19th century together with the Crucifixion group in front of the Cathedral.

Inside the cathedral, you will marvel at the huge octagonal dome and a richly-decorated Romanesque interior. You will see the gothic tombs of some of the Avignon popes. Some remarkable features inside this cathedral include a 12th century bishop's chair made of white marble used by Popes, two pipe organs, and a treasury of religious objects, reliquaries and vestments in the chapel devoted to John XXII. On the north side you will see the former Romanesque main altar. At the entrance to the Baptistery Chapel – the ante-room on the right – an early 15th century frescoes portraying the Baptism of Christ can be seen. A beautiful silver sculpture of the "Scourging of Christ" can be found on the north aisle.

Address: Place du Palais, 84000 Avignon, France

Phone: 04 90 86 81 01

Hours: daily 9am –noon and 2-6pm

Petit Palais

Built in the northern side of the Palais des Papes, this imposing structure seals the northern side of the place. This beautiful edifice was built during the second decade of the 14th century. Located on the Place du Palais, this is formerly an archbishop's palace. It now contains world-class collection of Italian Renaissance painting, including a transfixing Botticelli, as well as works of Carpaccio and Crivelli.

The palace was nationalized and sold during the French Revolution. It became a secondary school in the 19th century. Since 1976, it has been a jewel-like backdrop for the museum.

Address: Palais des archeveques, Palace du Palais, 84000 Avignon, France

Phone: 04 90 86 44 58

Hours: 10:00am – 1:00pm, 2:00 – 6:00pm

Rocher des Doms, Avignon. Photo credit: <u>Bradley Griffin</u>

Rocher des Doms

Take a leisurely walk uphill on one of the favorite strolling park on this part of town. Called the "Rock of the Monks", this is a steep outcropping behind the Palace of the Popes, overlooking Rhone River and Valley.

They said that the first human settlements in Avignon have been up here. This park was fully landscaped in the 19th century, shrubs and trees dot the place providing a relaxing ambience. Rocher des Doms covers 29,000 square meters of beautiful promenade offering a panoramic view of the surrounding countryside.

At the center of this park is a large pond with swans, duck, geese and carps. There is a snack bar where you can grab some sandwiches, salads, pizzas and hot snacks. Several beautiful statues can also be viewed here.

Address: 84000 Avignon, France

Phone: 04 90 80 80 00

Pont de St. Benezet, Avignon. Photo credit: Dan McKay

Pont St Bénézet

It's time to see the famous medieval bridge of Avignon. A lot of people may simply ask, why is this bridge, standing tall, proud and mighty, left unfinished?

This bridge was built between 1177 and 11 85. It originally spanned 900m across the Rhone River. The bridge collapsed frequently and was reconstructed multiple times. The early bridge was destroyed forty years later when Louis VIII of France laid siege to Avignon. It was later rebuilt with 22 stone arches which proved to be very costly to maintain as it collapsed every time the Rhone River flooded. Eventually, in the middle of the 17th century, it was totally abandoned. The four surviving arches were believed to have been built around 1345 by Pope Clement VI during the Avignon Papacy.

The bridge was built around the concept of a local shepherd boy of the same name. It also served as a worship place for Rhone boatmen until it became so unsteady and was deemed dangerous. Apart from the divine reasons, the bridge served a very logical purpose of providing a way to traverse between Avignon and Villeneuve les Avignon. The Rhone River on this part was difficult to navigate because of hidden sandbanks and many people drowned while trying to cross the river by boat. The new bridge at that time, saved lives, and enabled Avignon to control and levy a tax on the east-west movements of merchants, pilgrims, herders and armies.

Today, it is considered to be one of Avignon's famous landmarks, this bridge was classified as a World Heritage Site together with Palais des Papes and Cathedral Notre-Dame des Doms.

Address: Pont d'Avignon, Boulevard de la Ligne, 84000 Avignon, France

Phone: 04 32 74 32 74

Hôtel des Monnaies

This is one classic example of Italian baroque architecture. Marvel at its beautiful, elegant façade, loaded with details (angels, lions, eagles, fruit garlands, papal coat of arms and dragons) and characters from mythology.

This structure was built in 1619 and bears the arms of the Borghese family, as the Cardinal Paul V Borghese lived here. In the 17th century, this was Avignon's mint. Today, this is the home of the Olivier Messiaen music conservatoire.

In front of this place is a terrace always full of tourists. You may even catch a glimpse of the street artists performing before the crowds.

Avignon Town Walls

It's time to explore the historic walls of Avignon. These walls and towers or ramparts encircles the inner city spanning 4.3 km long. These walls were built in the 14th century during the time of the Popes meant to protect the city from mercenaries, mainly English brigands and pillagers.

These walls also served a secondary purpose at that time. It was meant to protect the city from the waters of Rhone River during periods of high water.

These medieval fortified walls certainly add charm and character to Avignon, mirroring the years gone by. And as you walk and explore the inner recesses of the city by foot, on crooked streets and leafy squares, medieval churches and handsome houses with ornate doorways, you will gain more historical discoveries that will enrich your mind and soul.

You may also explore the different shops tucked beneath the streets and alleys. Good buys are not hard to find which may prove to be irresistible.

One day of getting to know what Avignon is all about may not be enough. But then again, coming back will always be a most likely prerogative.

Let's cap the night with a dinner at **Cuisine du Demanche**.

Locals will definitely recommend that you dine at this family owned and run restaurant with exquisite interiors. Located inside the walls, they serve local cuisines using fresh ingredients. Savor French hearty cooking at its best! Atmosphere is contemporary with great service.

Address: 31 rue Bonneterie

Phone: 04 90 82 99 10

3 ARLES

Arles from the Arena. Photo credit: <u>decar66</u>

From Avignon, you can travel to Arles, the heart of Provence. With just 38 km in distance, you may spend a day in one of France's top tourist destinations. This is an important town, founded by Julius Caesar 2000 years ago.

The following are the estimated travel time from Avignon:

- 35 minutes by plane
- 20 minutes by train

- 40 minutes by bus

Arles is a unique and well preserved heritage site. Most of the structures and edifices here have been declared as UNESCO World Heritage sites. The whole town itself was able to maintain its old world charm. Romans have definitely made their mark in this historic town leaving concrete imprints on its architectural landscape. The most prominent of which is the Arles Amphitheatre and the St. Trophime Cathedral.

This ancient town lies in the Rhone south of the point where the river divides into two arms – the Grand Rhone to the east and the Petit Rhone to the west, then it flows through the Camargue, with its ponds and lakes, before finally going out to the Mediterranean. This is a place where you can see and feel the remarkable and distinct Roman influence in this Southern French province.

This is also the place of Van Gogh. Here, he found his inspirations and he was able to create about 300 of his masterpieces here. This Dutch post-impressionist painter lived in Arles in 1888-1889. Tales say that this is where he cut his ear (yes, you heard it right!) and gave it as a gift to one of the girls in a brothel.

Arles Amphitheatre. Photo credit: Wolfgang Staudt

Arles Amphitheater

This Roman amphitheater is the largest and most complete ancient monument in the town dating back 1st century AD. Built for an audience of 20,000, it once showcased gladiators and chariots racing. The façade has a double row of arcades with 60 archways. Seating for the spectators was once on 34 rows of tiered steps, the arena itself was built into the bedrock of the site.

After 2,000 years, bull games and bull fights are still being held here during the summer months.

Palace de la Republique

This place is located at the heart of Arles. You can easily spot its Egyptian obelisk (a tall, four-sided, narrow tapering monument which ends in a pyramid-like shape at the top) which stands at 15m/50ft high and fountain marking the center of the square.

It was first erected under the Roman emperor Constantine II. In the 6th century, the obelisk fell down and was re-erected on top of a pedestal soon surmounted by a bronze globe and sun in 1676.

These ornaments were changed in times of political regimes and they were finally removed and replaced by a bronze capstone until a fountain and the sculptures around it were designed by Antoine Laurent Dantan in the 19th century.

Other historical structures can be found here. On the north side of the square stands the Hotel de Ville (Town Hall) built in 1673-75. Its bell tower dates from 1553.

Address: 13200 Arles France

Saint Trophime Cloisters, Arles. Photo credit: Phillip Capper

St. Trophime Church

Another UNESCO World Heritage Site, this Medieval church with distinct Provencal Romanesque style was constructed in the 11th and 12th centuries. Trophime of Arles became the first bishop of Arles and this church was named after him. His relics were installed in the new cathedral around 1152.

One of its most prominent features is the 12th century portal which is acclaimed as one of the finest achievements of the southern Romanesque style. Recent restorations between 1888 and 1885 have made its quality and beauty even more transparent.

The theme of the portal is the Last Judgment, with "damned" souls being dragged off to hell on the right side and the "chosen" ones being delivered into the hands of the saints on the left. The tympanum depicts Christ in Majesty surrounded by the symbols of the Evangelists. Other narrative relics depict events surrounding the Nativity.

As you step inside the church, Gothic designs and architecture become more pronounced on the interiors. Typical Romanesque with thick walls and solid pillars can be seen. The ceilings are high with small windows set up above the level of the eyes. Over a thousand years, there have been many additions. Paintings and tapestries and sculptures with magnificent architectural details were added. Large oil paintings with gilded wooden frames and open pediments on top were installed.

You may also see the 4th century Sarcophagus – a funeral receptacle carved in stone which has later been transformed into a baptismal pond.

You should not miss seeing the Cloisters of St-Trophime that adjoin the church on the southeast side. Entrance is through a separate gateway to the right of the church façade. It is like an open air museum, a rewarding, peaceful place to visit with a meditative and prayerful atmosphere. Marvel at the columns and arcades with the finest and intricate details. The top of each column is carefully carved with elaborate capitals. These are definitely impressive work of arts! You can see statues of saints and angels on corner columns. Arches, pillars and columns are elaborately adorned. It is one of the most important cloisters in all of Provence.

Address: 12 Rue du Cloitre, 13200 Arles France

Phone: 04 90 96 07 38

Arlaten Folk Museum

Catch a glimpse of typical Provencal life back in the 19th century. This museum is housed in the 15th century Hotel Laval-Castellane, which stands on the remains of an ancient basilica. Founded by Frederic Mistral, a famous regionalist writer in Arles and a Nobel Prize winner of 1904, this museum showcases costumes, furniture, work tools, farming implements and objects of worship and superstition.

Address: 29 rue de la Republique, F-13200 Arles, France

There are a lot of other museums in Arles that you can just go and visit by foot. They display a lot of treasures from the ancient Roman periods which include glassworks, tools, statues, gold jewelry and pieces from the Stone Age. You will even see mosaic designed floors plus little models or replicas of the great European architectural feats.

Van Gogh Walk

One very interesting tour that tourists do in Arles is to retrace the steps or the memorable places where the famous artist of the 18th century lived, painted and died. Vincent Van Gogh spent his last and yet most productive years in Arles in the 18th century. He did about 300 drawings and paintings during those years. Ironically though, you will not find even a single painting of him in Arles at this time. In this town, Van Gogh set up his easels and canvasses to paint his most remarkable masterpieces. The Place du Forum, a major square in town is where he painted the "Evening Café", the Trinquetaille Bridge for the "Staircase of the Trinquetaille Bridge", the Rhone River quay for the "Starry Night", the Place Lamartine for the "Yellow House" plus a lot more places depicted in his several paintings. You can have the chance to walk down these places, where each stop has a lectern-style signboard with a reproduction of the paintings and interpretative information. The town of Arles is not that big. You can easily stroll up and down their little lanes, narrow streets, various squares and cafes.

Thermes de Constantin

Ever wondered how they bathed during those glorious Roman eras? You'll fairly have an idea how as you step into the remains of their Roman bathing complex which dates back from 4th century AD. It is situated on Rue D. Maisto in the north of the town near the arm of the Rhone River. This is a part of a once –extensive series of buildings resembling a palace. The baths were a famous social venue at that time and visitors enjoyed the luxury of underfloor heating. What remains today to be seen are the Caldarium (warm bath) and the parts of the Hypocaust (underfloor heating) and the Tepidarium (warm air room).

The walls, consisting of alternating rows of bricks and small worked limestone blocks, are built around a semi-circular apse which was lit by three high round-arched windows, and covered with a magnificent quarter-sphere vault.

Alyscamps necropolis, Arles. Photo credit: tpholland

Alyscamps

Just a short distance from the old town of Arles is a large Roman necropolis. This is one of the most famous necropolises of the ancient world. This site is of great historical and religious importance. This was Arles' main burial ground for nearly 1,500 years, used as a final resting place for affluent members of society in the medieval times whose memorials ranged from simple sarcophagi to elaborate monuments. From the 4th to the 12th century, this was a prestigious Christian burial ground, where several bishops were buried.

When the relics of St. Trophimus were transferred to the cathedral in 1152, it led to the demise of the necropolis. Today, tourists can visit the place and see its many tombs and gravestones which is a hauntingly fascinating sight.

Benedictine Abbey of Montmajour

In the northeast of Arles, perched atop a rocky hill is the Benedictine Abbey of Montmajour founded in the 10th century. It is a very important pilgrimage destination with an exceptional architectural ensemble. The Abbey is composed of a church, crypt and a 12th century cloister built by Benedictine monks. The place where it was built was originally a marshland. At the start of the 18th century, the Baroque buildings were constructed as the 12th century structures largely fallen into disrepair. The large plan drawings in the lobby will give you an initial overview of the entire abbey.

Address: Route de Fontveiville, F-13200 Arles, France

Admission: Adults: 7.50 €; Concessions (18 to 25) = 4.50 €; Free admission: minors under 18*; Free admission: 18-25 years old* (citizens of one of the 27 countries of the EU or are non-European permanent residents of France) * excluding school groups.

After a fully-compressed day trip, you can now spend the night in Arles then head to Aix-en-Provence for a day tour tomorrow. Or, you may opt to go back to Avignon and spend the night there before going to Aix-en-Provence in the morning via train.

From Arles, there are several bus lines which can take you directly to Aix-en-Provence.

The bus station (08 10 00 08 16; 24 blvd Georges Clemenceau; 7.30am-4pm Mon-Sat) is served by companies including Telleschi (04 42 28 40 22), which runs services to/from Aix-en-Provence (€9.80, 1¾ hours).

Long-haul, international bus company Eurolines (04 90 96 94 78; www.eurolines.com) stops here, though there's no ticket office.

Arles to Aix-en-Provence is about 74 km and travel time takes about 56 minutes to an hour depending on road and weather conditions, diversions and traffic plus other factors which may affect travel duration.

4 AIX-EN-PROVENCE

Fontaine d'Albertas. Photo credit: decar66

Aix-en-Provence is arguably one of the most beautiful cities in France. Aptly dubbed as the city of fountains, numerous fountains are scattered within the city intertwined with its old and majestic squares. More than 40 spectacular fountains help cool this city especially during the summer. Anywhere you look, you will feel the city's unique ambience and romantic character. Its leafy boulevards and public squares are lined with 17th century and 18th century mansions, accentuated with moss-covered fountains. This city became a center of culture under arts patron King Rene in the 14th century and was able to retain this stature until the present time. Today, Aix-en-Provence is a classy city of Provence and a prestigious student hub.

Aix-En-Provence Cathedral

This cathedral's origin dates back farther than the early history of the city. The beauty of this church encompasses a variety of architectural styles. It has a double nave, one Gothic and one Romanesque. A 16th century portal features elaborately carved doors. One of the historical highlights that you can see here is the 4th century Merovingian baptistery, an octagonal basin surrounded by a circle of 8 marble columns. This cathedral is also the seat of the bishop of Aix-en-Provence, thus his throne is here, a modern sculpture with wavy bronze panels. The altar is also an important feature which rests on three bronze shapes representing the Holy Trinity.

Market

Sunday morning markets in Aix-en-Provence. Photo credit: <u>Bradley Griffin</u>

Be sure to take time to explore the city and wander in its streets. Grab a coffee on the city's main street, the Cours Mirabeau and visit Musee Granet, Cezanne's studio and don't forget a visit to the open markets.

There are several markets and most of them are open daily but you may want to go and see the one at Place Richelme. Here you will discover vendors selling a variety of goods from clothing, antiques, local produce like fruits, spices, sausages, cheeses, plus a lot more. It is truly a remarkable experience.

Cours Mirabeau

It's time to take a relaxing walk along the Cours Mirabeau. Named after the revolutionary hero Comte de Mirabeau and was laid out in 1640, this is the central avenue with lots of grace and charm.

Fountain-studded, sprinkled with elegant Renaissance hotels and crowned with plane leafy trees, this place buzzes with both locals and tourists alike. Cezanne and Zola were aid to frequent and hung out at the places here, where bars, restos and cafés dot the sidewalks. It divides the old city center area and the university place and is often described as one of the most beautiful streets of France. This is also where you can stop for a while and have lunch on one of the many restaurants lined up in the street.

Cezanne

Paul Cezanne is a famous painter who lived and worked in Aix-en-Provence in the 18th century. His works and his legacy are very –well treasured in this place. You can retrace his steps and see where he ate, drank, studied, and painted by just following the Cezanne trail. These are marked with footpath-embedded bronzed plaques inscribed with the letter "C". There are informative guides to the plaques which can be picked up at the local tourist office.

Just like Van Gogh of Arles, though none of his original works hang here, it still pays to visit his studio which has been well-preserved and perched atop a hill. The studio was built on a land he bought in 1901 and is a must for any Cezanne fan.

Place de l'Hôtel de Ville. Photo credit: Andrew Lawson

Hotel de Ville

This is the central point of the Old Town. This is one of the prominent squares in Aix, with a great array of architectural styles, from the most simple to the more elaborate baroque style. There are a few monuments which borders the square. This is where you can also find the Town Hall, the Corn Exchange Hall and the Clock Tower.

5 BEST PLACES (EAT, WINE & DINE)

Dining in Avignon. Photo credit: jean-louis Zimmermann

Where to Eat

Avignon:

Fou de Fapa

This restaurant serves European and French cuisines. Claiming to be one of the best restaurants in Avignon, it boasts of straight-forward food and genuinely personalized service. They also use the best, fresh ingredients to whip up fine, delectable cuisines.

Address: 17 Rue des Trois Faucons, 84000 Avignon, France

Le Petit Gourmand

Craving for some delicatessen? This is the place to go. Try their Tapas, the Carpaccio of dry aged meat and the fois-gras ravioli. You may need to book in advance as the place is usually crowded.

Address: 37, Rue du Vieux Sextier, 84000 Avignon, France

Le Gout du Jour Restaurant

This is one restaurant that is getting good reviews not just because of the cozy ambience and delectable foods but also because of the price and the very attentive service that they provide to their guests. Some recommended choices are their crab and tomato soup, artichoke pancake and their apple-lemon sorbet.

Address: 20, Rue Saint-Etienne, 84000 Avignon, France

Arles:

Le Criquet Restaurant

This is a family-owned and run restaurant with good food, excellent service and great ambience. They are serving Mediterranean cuisines amidst a quaint, pretty setting. Foods are reasonably priced without sacrificing quality.

Address: 21 Rue Porte de Laure, 13200 Arles,

France

La Pergula Restaurant

This is a small restaurant close to Arena. They offer "al fresco" dining experience. They serve flavorful cuisines in a very relaxing setting. Recommended choices are eggplant mouse and baked goat cheese, bull stew and cod fillet, and not to be missed out is their lavender Crème Brule.

Address: 28 Rue Porte de Laure, 13200 Arles, France

L 'autruche Restaurant

They serve French cuisine at its finest with exquisitely prepared menus and well-cooked food from fresh ingredients. They combine impeccable service and a happy ambience. Guests say that this is French gastronomy in all its art.

Address: 5, Rue Dulau, 13200 Arles, France

Aix-en-Provence:

L 'Alcove Restaurant

Savor their fine quality French cuisine from a very sophisticated menu. This fabulous restaurant is in the center of Old Aix. They also have a fine wine list and they can definitely recommend best matches.

Address: 19 Rue Constantin, 13100 Aix-en-Provence, France

Cote Cour

They offer elegant dining experience in a lush winter garden overlooking the courtyard. A sweet atmosphere where creative Provencale and Mediterranean cuisines are served.

Address: 19 Cours Mirabeau, 13100 Aix-en-Provence, France

Vintrepide Restaurant

They offer local French cuisine. Guests are raving about their delicious food, great service and simple yet classic ambience.

Address: 48 Rue Du Puits Neuf, 13100 Aix-en-Provence, France

An Evening Out

Avignon:

Avignon is not high on nightlife although there are several places like bars and clubs, where you can go to just have fun, relax and unwind. There are even theatres which may feature live performances.

Bar Z

A rock bar which is open until 0130. This place is owned and operated by a rocker enamored by zebras. You can see this fancy reflected through the decors of this place.

Address: 58 rue de la Bonneterie, Avignon, France

Caves des Pas Sages

You can find this place in the south-east quarter of

town tucked away on a cobbled canal side. This down-to-earth bar is inside a wine merchant's store. Open every night (except Sunday) from 1800 to 0100, it offers a mellow atmosphere and local wines, plays jazz and blues in a laid-back setting.

Address: 41 Rue des Teinturiers, Avignon, France

Bokao's

Dance to the beat of electro and retro sounds in a non-stop party atmosphere. The setting is dressy and sleek. Open nightly until the wee hours of the morning.

Address: 9 bis boulevard quai St Lazare, Avignon, France

Arles has only a limited amount of nightlife entertainment to choose from. Most of the people here spend their night on cafés as there are just but a few bars in the area.

Café Van Gogh

This is Café la Nuit, thought to be the café painted by Van Gogh in his Café Terrace at Night in 1888. Painted bright yellow, it is always packed with dining tourists in front of its famous facade.

Address: 11 place du Forum

L 'Australian café Walla Beer

This is a popular place where you can grab a couple of drinks on a terrace overlooking bd Georges Clemenceau.

Address: 7 rue Moliere

Paddy Mullins

This is an Irish pub featuring regular music.

Address: 5 bd Georges Clemenceau

Aix-en-Provence

Unlike Avignon and Arles, Aix-en-Provence has a throbbing nightlife. There are plenty of pubs and clubs to choose from. There are even small theatres showcasing experimental stuff and less ordinary productions.

Tickets for most shows can be purchased directly from the venues or from the FNAC ticket network at the tourist office (tel: (04) 4216 1170). Available from the tourist office or you may check this link: www.aixenprovencetourism.com/aix-mois.htm.

Some of the bars are:

La Belle Epoque

This is a cocktail bar in a terrace setting. A great place to relax and unwind after a hectic day. They also serve meals.

Address: 29 Cours Mirabeau, Aix en Provence, France

La Rotunde

A classy bar with dimmed lighting, rich crimson décor, chandelier and mirrors. They also have regular DJs playing lounge, electro and disco music.

Address: 2Aplace Jeanne D 'Arc, Aix en Provence, France

The Hot Brass Jazz Club

A very popular place located in the outskirts of Aix, the club has been around for more than 20 years. They offer live concerts and high-caliber DJs.

Address: Chemin d'Eguilles, Aix en Provence

6 BEST PLACES TO STAY

Lobby of the Hotel D'Arlatan, Arles. Photo credit: erodcust

Avignon:

Luxurious

Hotel de l'Europe

This is the hotel who takes pride in serving luminaries from Napoleon to Jacqueline Kennedy-Onassis. They boast of excellent service and first-class amenities and facilities. This hotel is set in a 16th century building in the heart of Avignon and is just a few minutes' walk from both Palais des Papes and Avignon Bridge.

Address: 12 place Crillon, Avignon, France

Mid-Range

Hotel de l'Horloge

This is a 19th-century stone-walled hotel overlooking the picturesque Place de l'Horloge, in the center of Avignon. All stylish rooms have free Wi-Fi access. They are sound-proofed and are complete with all the amenities. Some rooms may even have private terraces.

Address: 1 Rue Felicien David, Avignon, France

Budget

Hotel Mignon

One of the best choices for budget accommodation with cute and comfy rooms. This is a boutique hotel situated in the heart of Avignon's historic center. They offer good service and modern amenities.

Address: 12 rue Joseph Vernet Avignon, France

Arles

Luxurious

Jules César Small Luxury Hotel of the World

This hotel presents Provencal and a monastic style.

It even has a cloister dedicated to Lacroix. Formerly a Carmelite convent, it is located at the center of Arles. It features a heated outdoor swimming pool and floral gardens. All rooms are fully-air-conditioned complete with first class amenities and facilities.

Address: 9 Boulevard Des Lices Arles

Mid-Range

Hotel d'Arlatan

Located in the heart of the historic part of Arles, this hotel is just a 2-minute walk from the Rhone River. They also have a heated swimming pool and en suite rooms with views. Decorated in a classic style, this hotel has a patio and a garden where guests can relax.

26 rue du Sauvage bp 60 109 Arles, France

Budget

Le Relais De Poste

This is an 18th century edifice which is formerly a coaching inn. Centrally located in a lively district in central Arles. The main sites are just a few minutes' walk away. All rooms are tastefully designed in Provencal style,

Address: 2 Rue Moliere Arles, France

Aix-en-Provence:

Luxurious

Villa Gallici

This hotel is elegantly decorated and offers sun loungers by the outdoor pool. It also has modern-day amenities and facilities which include a fitness room and a garden with furnished terrace.

Address: Av. De la Violette, Aix-en-Provence, France

Mid-range

Hotel de France

An old and charming hotel, it is ideally situated in a street parallel to Cours Mirabeau. It only a few minutes away from the famous landmarks of Aix.

Address: 63 Rue Espariat, Aix-en-Provence, France

Budget

La Beaufortine

This budget hotel will let you enjoy your vacation in the charms of a homey atmosphere. Only 5 minutes from the town center, it is very near the major destinations in Aix.

Address: 830 Route de Puyricard, Aix-en-Provence

7 OTHER RECOMMENDED PLACES TO VISIT

Lavender in Provence. Photo credit: Mike Slone

Roussillon

This village is situated in the Luberon, at the foot of the Monts de Vaucluse. It is surrounded by beautiful countryside and is considered to be one of the most impressive villages in France. Situated in the heart of one of the biggest ocher deposits in the world, Roussillon is famous for its magnificent red cliffs and ocher quarries.

Pont du Banc

This is the world's tallest Roman Bridge which served as an aqueduct that carried water from a spring in Uzes to Nimes. It took the Romans 5 years to build this structure which started in 1st century AD. It is currently one of UNESCO's World Heritage Sites. Such an amazing place and a great piece of architectural wonder.

Lavender Fields

The best season to see the lavender flowers in full bloom is from June to mid-August, depending on the area and the seasonal weather. In the Luberon and the Rhone Valley, these flowers begin to bloom mid-June. Wheat fields and lavender fields are found in the same areas as well as sunflower fields.

The classic view of postcard-purple Provence is found at the Abbey Notre-Dame de Senanque during summer.

Camargue – Rhone Delta

A sanctuary for flora and fauna, this is where you can find parks and natural preserves. This is a vast wetland spanning approximately 100,000 hectares, the largest in France. Here, white horses freely mingle with almost 400 species of birds including the pink flamingo which stands as a symbol for Camargue birds. There are plenty of outdoor activities that you can do here like horseback riding, hiking, camping, bird watching aside from plain exploring the nature/wildlife areas.

CONCLUSION

"La belle Provence." 3 days in Provence will leave you hungry for more. A few days will never be enough to explore this enticing Southern region of France however this is our humble attempt. The beauty and charm of Provence has sought its way into the hearts of many, bewitching and captivating them. It has been rendered and translated into words, painted into canvasses, sketched in notepads, captured in photographs, and most importantly, memoirs of Provence are forever treasured in their hearts.

The vistas are fascinating. Each town and city tells a story. One thing that shines through is the pride of its people. They are truly proud of their dramatic past which proves to be an endless source of inspiration. The architectural designs of the majestic buildings and structures in this region seem to have been designed to last forever. These encapsulate the historic character of Provence. This region is also the place of stimulating aromas and bright skies. Nowhere else is the scent of nature as magnificent as in Provence. Everything here seems to glow. Simply amazing!

3 DAY GUIDE TO PROVENCE

MORE FROM THIS AUTHOR

Below you'll find some of our other books that are popular on Amazon and Kindle as well. Alternatively, you can visit our author page on Amazon to see other work done by us.

3 Day Guide to Berlin: A 72-hour definitive guide on what to see, eat and enjoy in Berlin, Germany

3 Day Guide to Vienna: A 72-hour definitive guide on what to see, eat and enjoy in Vienna Austria

3 Day Guide to Santorini: A 72-hour definitive guide on what to see, eat and enjoy in Santorini Greece

3 Day Guide to Provence: A 72-hour definitive guide on what to see, eat and enjoy in Provence, France

3 Day Guide to Istanbul: A 72-hour definitive guide on what to see, eat and enjoy in Istanbul, Turkey

3 Day Guide to Budapest: A 72-hour Definitive Guide on What to See, Eat and Enjoy in Budapest, Hungary

3 Day Guide to Venice: A 72-hour Definitive Guide on What to See, Eat and Enjoy in Venice, Italy

Made in the USA
Coppell, TX
27 August 2023